Intimate Chronicles

Also by Christopher Middleton from Carcanet

Two Horse Wagon Going By
Selected Writings

Intimate Chronicles

by Christopher Middleton

CARCANET

First published in Great Britain in 1996 by
Carcanet Press Limited
402-406 Corn Exchange Buildings
Manchester M4 3BY

A CIP catalogue record for this book
is available from the British Library.
ISBN 1 85754 227 4

The publisher acknowledges financial assistance
from the Arts Council of England.

Printed and bound in England by SRP Ltd, Exeter

Acknowledgments

Some of these poems first appeared in *Columbia Magazine, Grand Street, The London Review of Books, The New Yorker, Oasis, Paris Review, P.N. Review, Shearsman, The Threepenny Review,* others in the pamphlet *Some Dogs,* published by Enitharmon Press (1993). 'Ballad of the Putrefaction' was also first published as a pamphlet by Carnivorous Arpeggio Press, 1993, likewise 'Fishing Boats at Assos,' 1994.

The picture alluded to in 'Egyptian in the Tube' is Balthus' 'Le Chat au Miroir III,' begun in 1989, finished 1994.

Contents

I

II

III

I

VALDRÔME GALLO-ROMAN

By people built as far as may be, in this bowl
Where eagles track the moves of mice, remembered:
The white cubicle, tiles to cowl an eave,
A bluish rose mosaic, in their haunt have lost

Contact with local crops, have little now to do
With wind, all through the night, fingering the pines.
Breathless figures broken from a patera,

Hearthstone cracked in a pocket underground,
Are good ideas: imaginary matter licked
Form into bronze that whangs on bronze no more.

That fatal daybreak passes in a flash,
Perfect, for its makings and unmakings
While you wet a toothbrush in the old stone trough;
So tasting a brioche, you wonder still what's what.

WAXWINGS ON A WORKDAY

Puffed oval by the wind
It rolls across our street:
A single silver bag an aubergine was in.

O visionary ladies, let your crimson frills
Swish about us, flick your fans, off your cheeks
Pick your curls while we are dancing.

It was silvered only by the sun, hollow skin:
The acorn belly of an infant, then miles, imagine
Miles of acorn-bellied infants, rolling, soon

Motionless, in puddles, their thin shit. Lined up
Along a branch the waxwings on a workday sharply
Lift their crests and call while we drive on.

VIEW FROM CUMBRIA, 1992

Frost silvering the fells, early light
Has touched a slope, consecrates
Mammoths in the distance, warm inside,
Matted Methusalems, now evidently sheep.

Body awake, felt them close, in a sweat,
For no shells had holed the stone house.
Then a frost spirit flashed out intact,
Through the window, quick:

Unbind the whiskey spell, quit the comfort
Of a land where Norsemen named some places,
And Serbian is not the tongue they curse in.
Frost early, light motion, sheep were lambs,

But who blew, before that, the battle horns?
Plundered hovels, torched the barley –
Who grinned when the shears cut throats?
Who poisoned wells, pissed on corpses?

All the way south, east, winging it
To where the new dead stiffen in ravines,
The selfsame body caught its breath, froze:
I will not starve this winter, or be shot.

THE WESTERN WIDOWS

Softly, widows,
You adopt
Euphemisms; the unloved
Contain their howl,
So it reddens,
Running rings around it,
Their skyline,

Haven't you heard
This? – meanwhile
Knock knock, and soldiering on
Poetry digs from
Time and more time
Its cavern, the global,
Echoing,

Lustrous nutshell;
Your horror,
There it slowly trickles in
To gleam with what,
Too long delicate,
You hardly thought you
Had to say.

UPON SAINT CRISPIN'S DAY

Aha, said he,
      Don't tell me you too
Keep somebody in mind,
      Who, when he squares,
On top of the heap now,
      His shoulders
To uncork
      Another wine bottle,
Holds his breath,
      Listens to the swish
Of arrows darkening
      The sky, and recalls
His forefather, the way
      He drew the longbow
At Agincourt.

PARIS

With a name like mine you will imagine
A long monologue to come, ruminative;
Not my style at all, I won't drone on.

It took two subtle moves to undermine
Menelaus, I won't say which. An easy target,
His self-will, strutting around in armor,
The bozo. Then to rip the web of that fine
Family, turds and torments underneath
The behavior they displayed at breakfast.

Imagine me, too, with historico-mythical
Vagueness: the lateral reach of my
Pectorals, articulate biceps, buttocks –
Me and Helen taking off, and the breeze
For once, among the islands, clement,
The flutter of my golden statuary hair.

Actually, folks, I am a stocky half-Hittite,
Dealer in used chariots and standard spears,
Hair continuous from my fringe to my feet,
Thick as garlic. The red of my tongue
When I talked of horses piqued her, somehow.
Made her breathe faster, her health improved,
Poor rabbit. If I knocked her over, so what.
The Greek idiot fell for my fantastic feet.

The pottery she brought along, I threw it out...
Hittite or not, she says, still you are number one.
Knit my brows, pretend I can't count so far.
There was a way she walked, true, and her grin,
Not her death-dealing smile, gave her away.

There is a queen for you, I told myself.
Relieved of ceremonial robes and the hoopla
She got into *poshlost* like it was wonderland;
Fawns and thinks small and does *pazarlik*,
Vile (as they say) and spiteful as the best,
So orphans can eat grass and men whack shields.

She took a liking to my feet, wide
As they had got by anchoring my behind
To a bronco. Forget the heartbreak. Wide feet
To walk avenues and kick horse ribs
Are what makes measurable this brute, life.
That was all she ever taught me: measure.
And a fat lot of difference it made,
Her la-di-da, a fat lot of difference.

BALLAD OF THE PUTREFACTION

The poem of hateful persons hot in his mind
He met the girl whose work was to roll in creosote
Himself he wanted to set fire to the hateful persons
Nobodies governing nations without any sense of what's what
Not victors but victims of their spooks and greeds

Those were to be the subjects of a poem which began
The moment he walked into one of their oblong hotels
He smelled the frowst of power they had left behind
People not born for power but victims of it
Who spray around the scene like tomcats their fear
The poem began but was interrupted by fresh sounds

A tongue moved in a sticky mouth and a snowflake fell
Those were calls from pigeon throats in the courtyard
This was a finger brushing the skin of a tambourine
These were the dawning sounds he heard
When the power of hateful persons first crawls in the dark

Himself had been interrupted by collecting impressions
The kind of work he would have been quarantined for
In a world controlled by the hateful persons
My work is rolling in creosote among carpets
The pools of creosote stick to my hair and skin
And my skin peels off when I wash the creosote away

Himself was interrupted by me when he saw me roll
He called me over asking why I had shaved my hair off
He gave me a fourteen dollar bill for the taxi ride
We should have supper he said at the Kim Kim
A Chinese Turkish restaurant on the lower East Side

So himself was interrupted by a girl with no hair
And the poem of hateful persons came to a stop
But still what made his flesh creep was their peeve
The smell of the "lounge" where they brooded destruction
The carbon script of a menu they ordered fishes from
The pop of a cork as it quit their bottle of Sekt
Fear in their bones fitting them snug in the world's night

Then the blackbird began to sing in the courtyard
For at first light still he did not sleep
Phantoms of hateful persons pushed their faces
Across the twilight between him and me
Again he saw the squat bronze tractor woman
Straighten her headscarf in the hotel garden
Their monuments he murmured their long knives
Hack out the tongues of nightingale persons
Their slug fingers sign contracts for weapons

Typically one who ordered a total change of trees
Resenting the way leaves tore loose from a sycamore
Himself too mumbled how their language formulaic and glib
Formulaic and numb and belittling gave rhetoric a bad name
Mouse gray their claptrap squeaking in machines

But we got along and my lips were clear of creosote
I only interrupted our long kiss to tell him You amaze me
If he forgot me it was the fault of a blackbird
Interrupting the poem of hateful persons at first light
Another moment and I will see him again
Free of his gang of hateful persons and police
He said they live secretly in fortified estates
And don't know beans about the hunchback in the belfry

So the poem will shine through air in the darkest places
So its voices will banish the fug they spread
Sunk in plush chairs or stiff at their tank parades

But again it is me the creosote girl who interrupts
We have escaped across many adjoining rooms
And arrive in a crypt where police wagons park
Waving our fourteen dollar bill we must fly on
Because the shooting will never stop it seems
Up and down streets we zigzag through fields of fire
He has told me he knows where the Kim Kim is
What if I doubt himself more deeply now than he can

SILENT PICTURE

There is a speaking nobody spoke of yet
Measureless an envelope of sleep
And all the speakers in it dreaming picture

We think we speak as anyone who dreams
Thinking he is awake
Speaks as if he were though he is not

Shrunken souls leap up and give a glory tongue
Complying with compulsion so to sleep
Flame perforates a cask or clay breaks wind

A speaker makes believe he is awake
Then horror stronger than the toxin
Speech secretes can desolate Dubrovnik

So the rat counts on the wall of his tunnel
A nightingale on air
Predatory tongues hit on a web of teeth

They may want to wag the web away but they can't
Picture on picture it is too thickly fraught
The tongues connect and weave it more and more

I thought I was awake and am asleep
Should I claw this way out of it
The dream I spoke will keep this picture silent

MISSING FROGS

Little frogs
why don't I hear you anymore?

This is your time of the year.
It was your custom to croak.

All though the night, the throb.
Spellbound, repetitive, too,

I was in the house, enslaved,
A frog should croak in deep water.

Your creek was dry, you were frogs,
not princes, I was never a slave.

Where are your needling, primordial
contradictions? I heard them.

Your cry carved the vast sparkling
zero, then, into triangles.

I went into your beaks.
You do not have beaks.

Far back I tasted, bitter,
the green, the prancing, emergence.

The beginning was before us.
There were no developments.

We were qualities of darkness.
I did go into your beaks.

Now I am in the air around the house,
distressed in the coil of your legend.

14

Breathe again, good cows, the scent of pear,
Moo approval, from your dewlaps lift
Your copper bells, and keeping time,
Do you shake them, loiter, see the people
Drink, frolic. Rifles cocked, the hairy

Partisans who guard this place
Fling their caps up, into nowhere, high;
It is not far, the cows, all their life
In rumination spent, they felt it
Not so far.

LEANING OVER

Leaning over this black
Cat of mine, my one and only
Familiar, nabob of the dark,
I gaze, gaze into his wild
Yellow eyes and think

He's part owl, see
The way he squats there, glossy
Gourd of a body anchored
Unblinking to this branch of ground.
Then why does he answer

Not owl, not owl
But a panther. Then why do I
Reprehend him: If so, some day
Mew and faugh, get educated, son,
Will be roar and howl.

Maybe, says he, but that's not
Quite the process. In our glowing
Midst the monster sits, your
Intestine hath many heads,
Ins and outs; insist,

As you will, on the reasonable
Head, you will not raise it
Beyond their magnet; turn its face
From blood's rage, from the ravenous
Intestine fist, and it shrinks,

Shrinks and is prone to forget, care
Not a hoot, toy
With its little time, spoil
Its intractable whereabouts, even
Twist, every which way,

Justice.
                    At this, taken aback,
I touch my familiar, call him:
Fallen star, street wise
Prince of latencies, adept
Of Sphinx, Medusa, Dragon, tell me

Why did you never go
With men, unleashed, on their walks,
Show them the cavern,
Unlit, where the monster
Waits for them, hopes for them?

Quoth now with a wink
The cat: I walk,
Mouse, nap as I please, but who first
Rigged gods, in their dynasties,
Then their catafalque?

Who measured his distance,
Split the rift and wedged
Monster into it? Who
Aims the pointing
Finger at himself?

THIRST CONFESSED

Face it, you are a little tired
Of the long trek to Troy;
Of other places glimpsed; of the fable
That our throb of time, first felt,
From sixty shrines
Illuminated earth with auras
Now being quenched by sixty lords of change;

Tired of retrieval – a lifetime,
In retrospect, might have clustered,
Detail on detail, round the taste
Of a cedar pencil bitten on a back doorstep
Opposite the great cathedral nave; tired

Of troubling anima for a sensation even
Richer, abrupter, than a madeleine.
All felt, all said and done,
Time is not a thing, nothing holds it
An instant still.
The long trek must go on,

And underneath the layered city, cool,
Below the rock any inscrutable event
Or silly habit warped, below folds in time
Idled away, or made something of,
A treasure hides, a shimmer comes to mind.

What is this mirage if not intent
To lift the shimmer up, give tongue to it
In a tongue its time has thickened
Into an apology for essential say-so;
Face it, or not, a negative will
Has all but bereft it

Of lustre, airy volume, now vague but rapid
Abstraction wizens it, a glance
Over the worn parapets of its features
Dizzies it, no voice responds
To voice voicing action where the action is,

Then to articulate the curve of a gaze
Winging home, as it glistens,
Captured at last
On its wings the shimmer,
For it has passed
Through the other eye of things.

1944

"Our lads have landed in Normandy,"
That's what he shouted. Scouring the pipes
Which propel time, I found them
There, nested in the scum, a figure and a phrase.

Brisk, waxed tips to his moustache,
A little Spartan thorn of a man,
Who in his singlet frogleaped, light
As a flame, across the vaulting horse
And sparred with elfin vim.

Sleep lost sight of, I make him
Shout again. Was it Sam Fox?
Voiced through the loon cry of valves
From pools, inlets, systems linked by tissues
Where hooded phagocytes in cells
Pump their polyphony through the dark,
The words trod out a rhythm, with its own
Weight each marked a notch across a scale:
Crazed Archilocus, now did he feel that way
Fish lines tug from footsole to fingertip?

Tudor oaks, the river Wye, the rosy castle
Reconfigure, out of atoms. Algebras of scripture,
So much gas before, prophesy,
Because a phrase has kept its cadence,
And Sam Fox is a presence, not a name –

Sam Fox who fought once through the slosh
Of corpses on the Somme, ducked through shellbursts,
Sang Tipperary, for the ping
Pong of the powers never was his thing,
And he forgot the Henries, thought Huns, calls out
His phrase again.

                              Barely awake his soldier boys
Attack the last yards to the mansion
From the stable we have slept in. So he stands
At ease, on gravel, at the oaken door, calls
Down crevasses where another tongue
Now takes their echo up,
Certainly, his weighted words. Ebert,

Sergeant Ebert was his name.

WARLORDS

The blackbird once believed
He cranked the sun up with his song

Likewise but with love
Quite inconspicuous women

Now the warlords crank and crank
Only graves come up

REMUZAT: LA COMBE

Four steps were a staircase
It smiled at me
In candlelight
As I took heart and mounted it

Worn down by years of feet
The stairs you see
I took a second look at
Like lips they lifted

Once the room had housed
A family of folks
Down below not far
On golden hay a flock of goats

Far enough I thought
From economic muck
And stuck with fond beliefs
Those figures on their thrones

Now a truckle bed
Here delights my back
Windowsill and simple desk
To prop my elbows on

Soon gathering in the dark
I heard goat bodies breathe
Long past the witching hour
A whole dead family talk

Across the screen of stars
Iconic jewelled unicorn
You drew their dusty hearse
Who now can know for what

With red wine awash
And a fellow feeling
Here I blow the candle out
Here I goat to sleep

OBJECTS MISTAKEN IN MUSIC

Hearing again the vowels of
That nightingale, darkly
Burbled in *The Pines*
Of Rome, and following them

The large brass starts to blow
From the ends of earth,
Columns of men, rivers proposing
An economics of empire,

First he hears no speech,
No crack of objects, roofbeams,
Only the onward slog of feet
And the wind, shuffling

Through umbrella pines, over tombs
On the Appian Way, and Rome –
Ropes creak hoisting cyclopic stones,
Fresh palaces of echo, a mason

Utters a grunt, captive Gaul
His groan, a Parthian head
Splitting open, ominous
The lull on a border pacified,

Et cetera, to the edge of time –
Hearing it, slightly smelling
African armpits, roast flesh,
Hearing the ultimatums, huge

Trombones herald the moment of truth,
French horns history,
And drums, the drums that mark
Moves of doom, the river's pulse,

He has walked across the kitchen,
Tipped from the old flower
Basket torn sheets of paper
Into the trash box,

The quest is on, for the fullest
Distant object in space without ceremony
Gone, which is here, if only
Only a ghost he circled the room,

Prosaic, took a stand
At his window, loaded
His Waterman, to start over,
Over again, for the first time.

CATACOMB

I only want to hear the wind in the sycamore,
To such a height it grew in the garden
Of that hotel, crumbled long ago.
I only want to see under the door the thin
Triangle of light from a lamp that shone
Day and night, in the passage, burnishing the walls;
Cool they were to touch, with an odd slant, inward.

Though I call out your pretty names,
I am afraid you have begun to forget me,
Crooked creatures now, propped against
This other wall.

                    And the creak
The window made when the wind blew,
Open window, that I want to hear;

And to think any thought whatsoever;
Time just enough to imagine it was I who said:
All your theologies, all, are fragments
From Aphrodite's shattered mirror.

THE OLD TOUR GUIDE – HIS INTERPRETER

He says there is a Greek house in Mustafapasha,
He says you go down a winding stone staircase
Into a crypt. On more stairs down to a crypt
Beneath it, a secret door opens. Now
There is more to be said, it seems.

I think he is saying that a blue sun
And utter stillness enfold the numen:
He says that in a third crypt under the second
A Christ of Sorrows stands alone, his face
Preserved in the original paint. That the face,
He says, illuminates all memory of the house,
Once you have been there, for your lifetime,
Is not certain.

What was he saying next? He says they found
A lost valley, by chance, two summers gone.
Conical churches there contain sealed tombs,
Full of treasure. Present, for anyone to touch,
A desiccated loaf, on an altar, a curled up
Sandal, each of a substance
Evidently shunned by mice.

Now he says there are many places
Not to be gone to. Memory has no desire
To be disappointed. But, he says, nothing,
Nothing stops you wanting to go there.

He is describing the valley, how across
Its clear stream, from one willow bush
To the next, singing warblers flit: the bird
Called popularly heaven bird can be seen there,
Crested, with blue wings, throat of rose,
Best heard at noontime when it flutes alone.

That is what I think he said. In his thick
Local accent now he is saying this:
You must not cut loose from here and now,
Both hands taking hold have to pull, he says:
Let the crypt call to you, as the long road did,
Let the valley track the turning of your eyes
And always haunt the here and now you see.

That is the gist. Wait, what wild talk is this
Of war striking a far country ...
                    Stored at home his great bow?
Seven times I heard the suffix
Which in his language indicates hearsay,
The saying a matter of doubt to the sayer,
Critical things might happen to have been
Otherwise.

                    Ah yes, he says,
Ah yes, this is the country of people after midnight;
Few have spelled out into the pleasure of a heartbeat,
Into a knot of mind, once and for all,
The loops of light they see spreading at sunrise,
The braid that snakes down a girl's bare back.
When we go to see what is there to be seen,
The knots and braids easily slip;
We learn to know how little we understand.

But as we go I believe he is saying
May Allah lift the griefs from all of us.

THE PARROT HOUSE ON BRUTON STREET, 1830

This very young man, face all flesh and bone,
Eyeglasses, gold and owlish, perch between
Parrots he peers at and his jungle brain. Those eyes,
So myopic they must blink to capture,

Accurately, screaming parrots, one by one.
In a keeper's grip, wingtip to wingtip,
They measure such and such; he is making moues,
Surely he mimes the volumes of their hornblack beaks.

Then while a thieving pencil sweeps up the crests
And down his own bent backbone strokes the plumage,
Turquoise, into place, people tiptoe in, to watch
Our artist copy the parrot he all but becomes.

Odder far he thinks these wicker bonnets,
Eyeballs which are beads, gnawed snickering lips,
Than they have deemed his amiable psittacids;
And look, now he delineates the people's noses –

Upon my word, how sniffily those humbugs behold
Not a "dirty artist" or "Wog's Robin" now,
But being tweaked, nothing to snicker at,
The organs of their own inquisitivities.

ZAGREB 1926

The window swinging open spread a flash
Of light, splendid and warm the sun
Settled on the table cloth, the vase,
Lay on the white bed, singled out the pictures.

Hallo, light, glorious with your rays,
Hallo, linen, fragrant in your wardrobe.
Flowering cherry steeped the orchard in perfume,
Bees occupied our thoughts, honey, the pure things.

Gentleness: back and forth it ticked
And talked, like an affable old man, the pendulum.
Gentleness: the clink of cups and plates,
The smells of cream and stored apples.

And while the slanting rays explored
Crannies where the light and shadow blent,
Our funny faces, caught in the globed vase,
And a snippet of our sky gazed back at us,

In its ample curves we contemplated
Birds that flew in flocks across the town,
The roofs of all the houses turning red,
Right above the bell tower, now, the sun.

(After a Serbo-Croatian poem, 'Reflections,' by Ljubo Wiesner)

SKATERS IN THE LUXEMBOURG GARDENS, 1909

Black on white, figures astride a frozen pond,
Long shadows travel, forms unfreeze the distance.
A clock high on the palace façade has stopped.
It is five to one, or else it is eleven.

Suppose there was that year no bombing season,
Though while snow drifts blew into Saint Sulpice
A ghost bicycled through them firing pistol shots:
However it was, here is a lull in a bubble.

Ankles turning as they try to move,
Two of the women wear such ponderous hats.
Shaping her mouth, narrowing her eyes
Another shoots an ecstatic look, at what?

Yes, a mouth can turn lips in like that
When ice absorbs a pond, air blows jawbones cold,
But *le dimanche* has arrived, the Galeries Lafayette
Set free their great bosomed girls.

Knees flexed and gliding from his corner
A waiter makes the scene, white shirt cuff
Circles the end of the longest arm on earth;
And the women giggle, this could be something else.

At the line of bowler hats behind them, not a glance;
Of the grudge fuming into the hat crowns, not a whiff.
Those bowlers heat old soldier headbones knit
In the semblance of a wound, raw, roughly sutured.

No use trying to tunnel back, they say.
Still you try it, drawn to any secret place.
Still the waiter fills his coat, not yet blown away
In a dugout; old fogeys crack a smile.

Webbed with hairlines the wafer of glass
Off which this print slid
Vaguely into the bluebell air of Spring in Texas
Eight decades almost after the event

Is in your lips, image intact;
The scratches hold their accidental ground
And are at home in the picture;
The people smile, humdrum in their hats.

Kin to them, rose Renoirs glow through the shell
Of the palace; air attends Fokine and The Firebird;
Five canvas women rolled under Picasso's bed
Have chosen who shall wear the masks and dance.

Yet unforefelt another ice was catching up on them.
Soon it will split even this mole's backbone.
Where do the long shadows else come from, and the light,
The sweep of light brightening that girl's face?

MONET'S 'WEEPING WILLOW'

Involuntarily
   Microbes
In a drop of water
   We see what they cannot

A carrousel
   The unbelievable
Speed of echoed
   Colors wheeling

And reel to seem
   To be seen weeping
Inside a single
   Unimportant tear

Or (duck in gunsight
   Fluting across the Danube
Delta at sunrise)
   A tot of eau-de-vie

Through its liquid
   Walls refracted
The cosmos calls
   Hallo goodbye

CONSTANT DANGER

Just now, in June 1994, and in Berlin-
Pankow where *Altstalinisten*, still
In the same old villas, deaf to the same blackbird,
Scowl at big blue TV screens,
I heard tell of a paper maker:
Old sheets from junk boutiques all over Europe,
Old camisoles, old shirts he collects,
Breaks the fibers down in tubs of wood,
Dries the mush, then fixes it, and presto —
Paper for etchings later to be hatched,
Labyrinths by fingertips invented.

      Still to be written, fit to be printed
On such paper, in letterpress, by hand,
The poem ruffled and warm as the sheet soon will be,
Folded and finely stitched
With gussets
Like the camisole a moment ago slipped out of
By a factory girl, who unpins in 1910,
Elbows up, her braid, winks to her image
In a fragment of mirror, quick now
She'll hop into her bed
With a frisky, shirtless printer

MIRROR RAP

This day the mirror,
Nothing in it,
Really nothing in it,
How does it do just that?

The touch
Of a rhythm and then
Skyblue the curtain
Hangs there, a fold of it,
Tubular, and over

The snowy wash-
Basin a
Platoon of stripes,
Too, the wallpaper,
Up front, lacy, light
In the oval glass;

But still the mirror,
Nothing in it,
Nothing contained, nothing
That brims. How,
How does it do that?

Where gone the creaseless
Pools of light, deep
Mirror-walled
Rooms through which
Like antlered
Stags the candelabras
Walk while, hyacinth-
Eyed, Rilke's
Brooding prototype
Gazes at the ooze?

Yet Pablo P. got
His whole thing
From what it did,
An oval mirror:

Outcasts, a guitar
Neck, a news
Flash (anarchist
Agitation), every
Bottle hollow, pipe bowl
Unfolds, quick
In the mirror, incised
By eyeballs, urgent as

Air from a windpipe,
Braque perhaps
Less flat, sensitively
Analytic, but
Puffier, even so

We are talking not
Myth, not art,
We're talking mirror
And nothing in it,
A nothing that acts
In the grease of evil,
The vacuum gobble,
Shrieks in the night,
Hating their lives, life,
The spoilers pronouncing,
Croak, croak,
Themselves the victim.

See it stepping,
A mirror people,
Down the street,
Sometimes tender,
Sometimes nasty,
A people killer,
That's the way
Today the mirror
Does it, does it.

THE GARDENER IN THE BASILICA

The gardener in the basilica, he stoops
To cut and lift the grass roots;
Little billhook in his grip he hacks what sprouted
Round the odds and ends at random:
Broken fluted column, writing,
A coffered rose, a marble sun.

While he cuts he whistles.
Same tune, over and over. Headscarf in the wind,
Down his back it flutters. Then he stoops,
As if born bent double. Face down,
He only sees a blur of marble forms;
He smells the wild pig smell of grass,
And smelling it he knows the weight of time.

Headscarf fluttering, hood of flame, fed by resin,
Color of the buried time, round his head,
Hidden in it.
Never to be restored. Timbers creaking,

Low in the water, black on violet, home,
A galley anchors. Fingertips have tooled
In hammered gold an olive leaf. Deer leap
And the dolphin. Likely tales
About a god
Born flesh and bone taunt the peregrine soul,

And him, robed in his dust, perilous
Round his head that long
Gone Ionian autumn, him hacking,
Stooped, whistling, over and over
The same tune.

FISHING BOATS AT ASSOS

1

Goodbye bastions Aristotle squinnied at:
Over the hill I have to go, scorched
By a thought for the purposeful
Multitude building you, and down to the cool
Spread shadow of an ilex, phantom, no,
Barbarian to your bronze people.

                          Goodbye
Delight among the drums of stone,
Once temple columns being lifted up
To civilize your mammoth headland –

                   And from her cabin,
Softly speaking, a girl steps, white lace
At her fingertips.

2

As ash flies from the tip of a cigarette
Into the harbor water
Moon on moon has risen and will set –
                        They disappear,
The purposes; we disappear
Among the gunwales, capstans, grunge, lapping;

Lemon crescents on their scarlet,
Flags droop, solitary lights – flicker of a look,
How many smokes ago,

First a shock, then a script
Hook, line, and sinker penetrating you –
Sprint across the water. So does love.

3

Steady now, snowy in arc-light
The loop of a gnat
Did not collapse the model of its whim,
                          A shooting star.

Purpose begins when a blind will takes
A hold on time, toils then to perfect
An image of its matter; aspires in good faith
To provide; persists through loss,
Must keep going till it melts into mind:

Süzül oynak dalga ...

                          Drifts of time,
Heaving poison cake, layer on layer,
                          Secret in the seen –

Tell me, Lord, to walk to you across the water

4

Canopies flap again, to fresh paint on a prow
The moon tries to pin a medal; the harbor
You could cup in a hand forgets for a minute
How distant, how old it is: everything ripples,

Dazzles, gives. Next, the phenomenal
Winking fabric clicks shut, and, trapped,
A mole thought can mutter only
"Hallo, now here's a thing."

5

                 A surge of joy
Suddenly remembering a blue light,
The shiver of it over the scales of a mackerel,
Warmth of an oar gripped
By fingers far bonier; then curious
Warrens you dug with tooth and claw
In sand; and freshest –

                 The first morn makes pristine
Bastions glisten;
Ovals of air flute one huge
Here-we-are hosanna with a scent
Of bread and woodsmoke,
Pinewood and excrement.

6

                 A silver griffin
Struck into a tetrobol, forepaw raised,
Passes from hand to hand:

Where now, with knapsack and Cannon,
Barbarians crawl, a history disappears,

So a soul's
Random misgivings can
Disappear, detach, for wishing on,

                 A single star.

7

Complete their letter O they cannot,
        The sheer strakes, though
Hulls float, signs roll, cluster
        One by one, and point:

Only their being mirrored, mirrored being
        Can make a little fishing boat
Named Pure Ellipse, complete a melon segment,
        Say, untoothsome rind,

And find a globe. The mirrored boat, on zero,
        Surfaces, neither
Boat nor surface, but a canopy spread
        By the whirl of an *axis mundi*

Burnishes deep silence, bids midget words
        Dance in a last light
Where engines chug and loud all night on a roof
        There were seven voices,

Storms of laughter, stories, language,
        Rough-hewn, another bastion
Canopied the mirroring. Notions, move over:
        Those were the boatmen.

A LANDSCAPE BY DELACROIX

They said shadows unrolled, or more precisely
That trees unrolled their shadows.

Don't believe a word of it: no sky,
No sun at all, but those trees have toppled
Across the slope not even shadows, but savage,
And so intent they have discredited the sky,
A stuff, it might be treeness, a cascade

Of rough bark tearing your fingertips off
In a collapse of earth,
If ever you noticed, in the instant, nerve: plotless
Light inscribes, toiling with its rays,
Protozoic spirit, to stir up

Cool deposits, first a formal blur,
Then this paint you'd like to gallop across
If you were a large French horse, unshod:

Murk, a blot of aquamarine spilling out of it,
Dashed trunks, five, in the foreground –
You missed the squish of the small brush inking them in,

But no matter, the thing speaks, a backbone
Hurting, flayed, the light's body a human sees with love,
Opening a mouth in horror at the moon.

MUSA PARADISIACA

(on a painting by Jean Bouchet)

The muse of paradise is a young banana palm;
Nipped by one blizzard, she
Grows back again. Her branches,

Are they bole or leaf? Both: a peacock
Green feather bathes, rippling upward
In shadow, in sharp light –

Shadow from above, light from underneath,
As if anyone remembered now
Which is which. She is Lethe also:

Love as you may her poise, she nods
In a space behind time, and shows,
In a time behind space, how hotly,

Drilling through potent indigo, a never
Agitated rhomb of rose
Burns. At that core her fingery quill

Points, to disclose goal and path. Whereas
Absently she models, in a wave,
Shadow – stepped bars of a moroccan

And apple green, her rose rhomb marks
Peril enough to draw, catching his breath,
Anyone, eagerly, in.

BERLIN: MOMMSENSTRASSE 7

– for Joachim Sartorius and Karin Graf

Antiquish tiles in a house on Mommsen Street
Line three walls of a demure retreat:

Blue bees seem to ride the backs of butterflies,
Rocks ring a pool, a warbler perches there;

Grouped in fours the figures count as pairs,
Except for threes of sulphur yellow daisies –

Those daisies: All around three walls they sprout
To polarize the green of rushes. While you pee

There's time to look around. One square in three
Reiterates the warbler, swallowtails with blue

Anomalous bees riding them pickaback.
Sore eyes take their delight in such a scene,

Bladders groan with relief, to be releasing
In the round presence of a rustic pool

Their pints or quarts of silvery alcohol.
So folks rejoin, refreshed, the wag of tongues:

While conversation buzzes, wild, in rooms
Vastly more spacious, memory retains

The imprint of this cubicle – a theorem,
Secret, of tiles combining elements in twos,

Except for daisy triads, which are solar sprays,
Except the warbler singing, solo, in the reeds.

All systems finally crush the worlds they shape,
Hydraulic or political they flush our lords

Dionysus and Apollo down the drain;
Some figures out of nature yet remain

And flit, unhopefully, around the pool.
The rising wave, will it be bombers or dragonflies?

Now for a time restored the simple john
Commends what folks complect to keep them going on.

A PICTURE WHICH MAGRITTE DEFERRED

Lookee from the garden
Papa in the window
Dandles our baby

Thinks it is a telephone
Nope it is a baby
Beaming in the window

Beaming our baby in
Earhead footpiece
Mighty like a telephone

Harkee baby sapiens
Billboards in the metro
Plot your new career

Solving global problems
Megabuckaroo to be
Proud homo sapiens

Working with your body
Welcome this mutation
Papa points the way

Internet chromosomes
Acronyms and digits
Impact his labyrinth

Telebaby Faustus
Floppydiskiades
Whelp of the Netherworld

To your cordless baby
Papa in the window
    Snuggle up and babble

    Lookee in the garden
See us gnomes
    Grinning from the marigolds

ON A PHOTOGRAPH OF CHEKHOV

– for Katharina Wagenbach

While the rain comes pouring down,
Chekhov, in his white peaked hunting cap,
And prone beside a rick of hay, surveys
The scene behind the camera, narrow-eyed.

While in Berlin the rain comes pouring down
And will refresh the yellowed centenarian
Blossomer in the courtyard, Chekhov has
Anchored his umbrella, gone to earth.

Ivory handle of the slim umbrella shaft atilt
To birch trunks in the background, has a curve;
Eyesight arching clean across the image
Divines, in the cap's white crown, a twin to it.

Chekhov's brother, meanwhile, props his head –
Summer rain, phenomenally somber –
On Chekhov's hip; from his blubber mouth
A howl escapes, the sockets of his eyes

Are black, as if he wore, beneath his bowler,
Smoked eyeglasses; as if he were, perhaps,
A horror Chekhov carried on his back, and still
The rain comes pouring down, and the umbrella,

Hulk become a dome to shelter Chekhovs, both,
Can float across a century, be put to use.
O perishable hayrick! – and its fringe,
Where Chekhov tucks his knees up, will be damp.

Yet Chekhov's massive cap, laundered a day ago –
Intent beneath its peak his eyes are watching
How people make their gestures through the rain,
Set dishes on a table, turn

Vacant faces to the window, wring their hands,
Cling, so predisposed, to their fatal fictions,
Or stroke the living air, to make it hum
With all they mean to talk about today.

THE EXECUTION OF MAXIMILIAN

1890 already, or almost, and not later. This is the room. This is where … Méry Laurent received Mallarmé and Gervex. This is the room in which they were photographed. (Stooping hooded behind his tripod stands either a hired professional or Dr. Evans, Méry's protector, whose diagonal gaze used to rake the interior of Napoleon III's mouth; or else, having shot a last glance into Napoleon's mouth twenty years ago, near enough, Dr. Evans had already quit the scene.) First it is Méry we see, sitting at her grand piano. Her hair looks blacker, sparser than it should; by all reports it was a glossy torrent, honey-colored. We see Mallarmé, his goatee now whitening below his underlip. Standing behind Méry he lunges at something, an emotion, one arm extended low, as if to evoke the buttock absent from all the bloomers. We see Gervex, who leans forward, arms crossed on the back of his chair, gazing at Méry, a grizzled profile, short legs and bony knees in pinstriped trousers. The two big windows are shut. Because there are roses on the piano, it might be Spring. Do these people, with their aching heads, only feel at home in sealed and riddlesome rooms? Deep pelmets overhang mushy drapes of velvet; or is one small window open, after all, for outside, strangely suspended above and behind the small head Méry tilts, coquettish, in mid-air … Mexican riffraff in French uniforms are shooting Maximilian point blank. Maximilian stands between two thieves, who are generals and are also being shot by their riffraff with French rifles and French bullets. Maximilian is wearing, while the bullets riddle his torso, a tall sombrero. That is what seems to be going on, that is where the action is, in the air outside, on this dark artistic evening. Back inside the room, everything is contained, except the perfume. In a glass hutch the bric-à-brac is contained; in a heavy damask cloth the piano; contained in heavy frames the diminutive paintings on the panelled wall, many by Manet. Even the sofa is contained in the skin of a lion, the people in their clothes, the mirror in its ornate gilt; and hung over the mirror, so that she may see her beautiful face, a portrait of Méry slopes, blurred, containing in its invisible back an oblong hardly less negative than the azure zero which still haunts, still excites Mallarmé as he lunges, extending an arm. The oil contained in tall brass lamps is so pure, so still, the wicks it feeds ("humects") do not smoke as the rifles are still doing while Maximilian discovers that the Bank of France has decided to drop him. The tallest picture, at which nobody is looking, can be identified by the lion man. Inhabiting the bottom right hand corner of the only section visible, he scribbles with a white quill an elegy, perhaps for his skin which contains the sofa. Above the disappearance of Maximilian and his thieving generals in puffs of gunpowder smoke floats, or is hooked, a decomposing bird of paradise. Under so many eyelids, the roses on the piano, fresh, presented with a smile by Mallarmé, pretend to be nobody's sleep. They will be trembling when Méry turns back to the keyboard and concludes the evening with a spirited hat dance.

SMALL CARVINGS AT ARYCANDA

Not much is left:
Like a bubble with a cleft
At twelve o'clock, a flying heart
Floats from a stem, which stoops
As the stem of a bluebell does.

Somewhere else, an inch or two
Above the ground,
A cluster of grapes, diminutive, hangs
Bursting from its marble slab,
Halfway liquid in your mouth.

All this, equally for the poor:
On several tombstones flying
The bluebell heart, lightly weighted,
And on a sunken slab
Clustering grapes that call

To be caught in the cup of a hand,
To be fondled, every one,
By the flesh of a fingertip,
Till bud can bud no more
And spurts its grapeness out.

Hyperbole, no doubt. How else
To feel the flash and throb afresh
Two hands, a little hammer,
And a blade of bronze
Divined in the dead stone?

How else to breathe again the life
Of carnal imagination working as a hinge:
The door the dead saunter through
And the living rush at, opens:
Here heart and grape mark

The narrow rapids where they meet
And spirit streams, making faces.
Gently now, nervous as the nostrils
Of a unicorn, or, come to that,
Of a gundog, the signs explode

Our electric shellac myths
Of Madonna and all that rot:
For a minute the bilge of our kitsch
Ebbs, heart beats
And the grapes come out on top.

EGYPTIAN IN THE TUBE

The usual rumble of the doors
And at Swiss Cottage in she steps.
I should have seen, there and then, her face
Of golden bird, but it was plain
Until, a picture in my hands,
It flashed upon me, golden bird, at Finchley Road.

Yes, the toes a little splayed
Placed on the border of a Cretan rug –
Rose pyramids at first, but then
Cuneiform wedges, very red;
And up and up to the second foot, there
She put it, on a cushion, sat erect,
Capped in hair which glistens like
The plumage of a predator:

Enormous glance of eyes directed at
A mirror's back, intent, I mean the gaze,
Horus-Eye, it was the apex of
A triangle the fingers of one hand
Had mounted on a base
The other hand, her left, drew taut,

And knotted round her tiny waist she wears
An emerald, ordinary sweater trailing
Down across her danskins at the groin.
As if about to run, the glance, the poised
Seventeen-year-old and lithe
Presence, in a split
Second she'll release the arrow, yet
Spellbound she poses

Housed in a web of triangles crisscrossing
A rhomb that slopes the other way –
An ottoman festooned with rugs of wool,
Pink, to crescendo in the Cretan wedges.

She held the mirror for a cat
To see whatever, perched on fur,
A cat might see in a mirror:
All you saw was the cat's golden eyes,
They shot a horizontal to complete
Another triangle, for her hair is parted
Right above her nose, a line descends
To the spread-toe foot and ricochets
Off one toe's tip,
Past the other foot's contour,
And up to where the cat begins
To hump its back.

When I stood to leave, doors rumbling open
At Finchley Road, I saw no less a marvel:
Opposite, Egyptian in the Tube, my neighbor,
There she was, one shoeless foot
Arched on the nondescript upholstery,
The other on the floor. Golden bird, she looked
Me up and down; I had become
The mirror in her hand; I was her cat.

We closed the book, and it was over.

III

SOME DOGS

Hereabouts there was a time of day
When the dogs came out of doors
Content to lie down in a garden.

Autumn's first cool, streets refreshed,
Flesh more than ever willing –
The clouds whiffed across the sky, so pink;

So blue the sky it was a cup of delphinium.
Somewhere else, poplars and olive trees
Were turning into a silver screen, so fast

People walking past them, with a scythe
Or sack across their shoulders, wore
Inexhaustible liquid outlines.

There too the dogs rested from their work.
Wild rabbits breathe again, gazing at space
In his café the old man mutters "fils de pute."

A gap in the bush gives you one more chance
Now, when the dog walks from his house,
To hear the breath expelled as his body meets

The ground, to see him crook a foreleg, fold
A paw to rest the back of it on earth, and tuck
The pad beneath his breastbone. He looks around,

One thought obliterating in that instant
Every single smell or sound in his neighborhood:
My dish was full, now I have licked it clean.

OAKS NEAR COLUMBUS

Oak I can see
    An enormous, never quite
Tightened knot, implies
    All trees in eyeshot;
Solid they stand their ground,

A pasture, flat, and from
    Such a maze in space
Oval eyes exact
    Hither and anon a whispering;
Every this is evidence of its that,

So the several branching
    Depths of trees recede while they
Stand firm and betray nought,
    And grieve not:
One of their kind, this Columbus

Oak I think, its knot
    Being now
Stilled by their motions,
    Loosened, though never quite
By their grace.

WINTER SUN FLOWER

ψυχῆς ἐστι λόγος ἑαυτὸν αὔξων

-Heraclitus

Beside the old red pepper stalk
I lopped,
Hardly thinking the earth
In its pot
Could bear more fruit,

Stem on a diagonal,
Terribly thin,
Pointed leaves grew from it
In separated steps
You could never tread on,

Bent with growing
Now between the balcony
Bars a yellow
Head opens, the black
Bed of seeds

Reflects and for a time
Slowly rising to it
Still glistens
Without winking at
An unknown sun

ALONG A LEAF

A leaf on a branch somewhere,
A mountain road, leading off,
Leading off, that's all;

A leaf on a branch anyone could crawl along,
Rounding the leaf, then dropping off,
Dropping off, that's the thing.

Before the great gate of Baghdad creaked open,
At sunrise, Layard had a while to wait.
Shoeless, stripped, what was he thinking of:

I am done up, now bless you, my friends,
Brave bedevilled Bakhtiars,
Worse off than us, fierce in your ways, unorganized;

How many months more will I be on the move,
Smelling alien dusts, the top of my head
Reading the signals of roseblue sky;

Learned alien tongues and smoke; unrolled
Among scorpions my carpet;
Crawled free of the leaf and came to be me;

And recognizing him, while, spellbound,
Gracious, and breathing as usual, English folks
Rode out through the gate, Ross to Layard said:

What happened to you? By Jove, Layard,
Whatever happened to you?
And that was all, and Layard took a bath.

A beak on a bird, all bird, for beyond
Its tip a bird space, conclusive,
Will pocket a scrap of food, a greaseless warble;

Or in Asia, not yet absorbed by the parade,
A hole to vanish through, that's all,
And come out on the other side of the air

In an ordinary place, astonished:
People you wanted to be with, gathering there,
Drink their tea from glasses, talk nonsense;

And here is the ordinary mountain, not mapped,
Here, unknown, saying as usual yes,
Simply a clear blue sea.

DUNA WINE

It is red and glass
    It has properties
        To be seized upon

Not by guesswork
    Not by familiarity
        Abstraction saps you

And the thing itself
    Expires into air
        A stupefickle music

Analogy streams from it
    Danubian deviations
        Bend perception's conduit

Any object looked for
    (Even little texts –
        "Product of Hungary")

Has a yen to be distant
    But to be pulverized
        Being waved away? No

To resist or position it
    Let me make sure this time
        A round rim a circular base

A stem going up and down
    A red a glass a pool
        With ellipses intersecting

(Six for counting now)
    Transparently "hand blown"
        Very like an animal head

Sort of tickled along its
    Electric jawbone
        A fingerprinted infinite

Yes red no furious tilting
    But in the glass a breath
        Bubble marks the exception

Here the uncontainable hid
    To know it in fear with wonder
        Then to perceive how I am

THE GREEN LEMON

Seen to hang in a lemon tree
A solid emerald lemon

Unremarkable a lemon hanging
In a lemon tree

Pulling at the stalk
The weight of the lemon

One thin brown hand will reach up to pick it
Thin brown hands drop into sacks ten thousand lemons

Inedible as the weight of the lemon
Tough peel of its glossy pod
Hanging by a stalk in the lemon tree

Unremarkable inedible tenacious and primitive
Rondure of one preponderant lemon

Under the gun ten thousand lemon pickers
Will pick from earth's axle of fire
As bread the lemon and as rent in cash

Preponderant and inedible
So many thin children in a ring around it
Primitive but loaded
Unremarkable but coming to be delightful
The hanging in itself of the green lemon

Like other lemons ripening dull
It hangs all alone
Regardless of hanging lemons
The sun and the moon
Object of thin unremarkable hands
All alone it hangs and has gone dull

BICKERSTETH

Raccoon scuffle in the roof, and music –
Oboe, goldfish, bubbles of a glockenspiel –
Before a fifth sip, silent at first
Memory pays a visit.
                                   No obstacle
The prudent footstep overhead, or you,
Wine glass, while I thumb
Off your rim a residue of olive oil:

For then he would, with snowy lint,
Wipe the rim of the silver chalice
Before we sipped our sacred blood across it;
Barely a sound when his black shining shoes
Are seen to sidestep, on to the next
Opening lips, among the tombstones.

Pearly in the oyster church a swirling nova now
I construe him, though for umpteen years
I never heard the candlewick behind him
Crackle so.

                   If the acidic cells that uncongeal
Oblivion, now and then, had not been matter's long
Laborious design, now I would not see again,
Always brushed so neat, his silver hair. Master,
Never a bugaboo, aeons before Drakul
Took to the screen, he flew, rustling in his gown
Through the long gallery.

                  A man without malice,
His authority, when I was watchful, fought
Another for my wits:

His, of a temperament easily generous, not
Thwarted by craving, therefore easy on power;
But when the other, a peacock, displayed,
The magnet of one shriek pulled from rosebush
And chimneypot a wet fur smell; then mystery
Drenched in bitterness, every Spring,
The east lawn.

Privileged by his long,
Symmetrical, Norman jawbone, our master,
Servant when he tilted the chalice to our lips,
He showed, blind as we were, how Latin
Crossed tortuous destinies, gaps dividing us
But not the gods, and could be muttered
Sometimes, in a twilit church,
Recondite as ocean cradled in a grotto,
Sometimes simply etched on air by shepherds' tongues.

He lived on a hill, far off;
You went there, in my anticipation, once,
Equally old, handblown wine glass. To that
Wrinkled mother of his
Who gave me tea and bread,
Now you bring a full flagon:
A salute to his reverence,
And to her discarnate bones.

THE LIME TREE

Thank you for giving birth to me in the first place,
Thank you for delivering me from the dark,

You whose round arms I stroked with feeling
Made presence atmosphere and contact known.

And I wanted not that Englishness;
I wanted deliverance from you so soon,

From the sticky stuff you weltered in,
Leaf, branch, and bole in your shade they dispensed

The glue, the fragrant glue, but your blossoms,
Lady, they did provide the pleasure of tea.

You stood in your own glue, fascinated,
Stirring soup, mothering lambs, telling your sex

Hush, don't you bother too much about it;
It, it, the enormous poison tree, once fire,

In your conscience you capped it off, mere fume;
In hope that hurt might never occur, defensive,

You dreamed of hoopooes perching in your crown,
Drenched in your glue for ever their crests of rose:

So the maternal shadow works mischief with men;
Their quarrels rumble first in the glue cocoon.

Now you sleep, sag-jawed, in your wing chair,
Doped, breathing steady, life will not let you go:

You who could see the colors in every back street,
Who told the stories, magnifying into marvels,

Detail on detail, the turns and twists
Of happenings that never were not nice –

Game old chattle who never peeped over the rim,
Who less than once in a blue moon could scream

Uncongealing, suddenly rid of the stuff
Your civilization spurted over you, glue

Twinkly as the round of talk you spread,
Lawn sprinkler, swivelling over shorn

Tips of grass blades, while our wrinkled lips
Sip tea in the bosque it cools.

For sure this line is not easy, but it must out:
Lime tree, your fragrance called me, always

Tenderly, back, but on, on I had to go, not
Looking for anything, but at every thing for the sign

That flashes up-down, lightning bolt, a blade
Cleaving the creatures, glued from crisp.

I was for the owls, for hornets, for nomads,
For such fools as never knew they were honest,

Who have wandered far, to come through,
Who have bitten their way through,

Who have learned what it means to be altogether
Alive, unattached. Of nippled hard

Breasts to be sucked, of glue
Twixt lustrous thighs, of moisture

In the mouths of girls I did not speak,
For it is all glue. What now am I on about?

Who? A creature who cares to come by,
A silvery one, brisk, with her own story:

Sixteen, with a child who walks before her,
While in and out through quick disguises

She who shimmers has to slip.
"See this headband?" A motto on it.

"Now you read it," and I could, it said:
"Not one day's help from anyone."

Here she shimmers mercy through my thick sleep,
Gives me her hand, and it is flesh,

Looks at me, leaves me, with what her look can give
She lifts the glue, all of it, out of me.

RESISTANCE

Crow soon, rooster,
Let there be time to remember now
For Mohammad
How in the blaze of day we walked
Up the mountain –

Red earth, white stones –
Walked up and up
To the spring, under the fig tree
And drank
How sweet, how cold

And down again
Admiring the sea haze
Soon he will start to whistle

Through his teeth, and still
Softly whistling
He dances for a minute
And has forgotten
To be walking
So he danced the heat as it moved him

Arms lifted among the pine trees,
Foot lifted, bending a knee, one dusty
Toecap traced

(On white earth, red stones)
To no end, a flickering loop,
For him I can remember
Nothing of his ancient
Ghost of a tune, only

How he let go, gnarled flesh worked thin
Cascaded from his collar bones
And swayed to join the circle
The minute
He felt that way.

NAKED TRUTH

What I really wanted to say, I could not:
Animals wear their clothes all the time.

Waking up in the night I find the cat
Has woken up less than a breath before.

So he was waiting to go out into the dark;
He knew the exact moment I would let him.

There are things he knows by his silence.
If he meows it is because he knows

A person expects of him some kind of speech.
Among cats he will only hiss and spit,

And he keeps for himself the purr to relieve
And grasp, one breath at a time, his servitude.

When one front paw lifts, the other three pick up
The tremble of labyrinths alert in other rooms.

What beckons other cats out from behind walls?
It is their sinews hearing those three receivers.

So air in a painting links acrobats or bottles.
So silence walks in the connected fashion of cats.

There are things he knows by his silence;
I would like to speak in his clothes.

A BREEZE IN DERVENI

Avoid time. The topic
    Is all husk. Think of a green
        Window. Imaginary air. The squall

Hit, sand, in seventy three,
    Grains of it blown aloft
        Fondled her face. The indigo
            Gulf a cauldron, hot Greek

Meat, the reek of it, crisping.
    Capillary, but Pliny's,
        An oak was vocal – then a
            Lacework of limbs, never quite
Knotting. The woman of Delphi.

The woman of Delphi crowed:
    My son in the photo … No mistake,
        His eyeballs, jaw, collarbones
            Melt into those of the bronze
Charioteer. Times,

Times connect, the hubs clash, a spark shower
    Floodlights ouzo,
        Octopus, a frisbee cleaving
            Twilight in the haberdashery:
Open the window

Wider. Snowy muslin
    Curtain puffed
        Dwindles like a chrysalis; it is cooking up
            A storm; inshore the *méduses*

Float – soon she will shake out,
    Into the breeze, her hair,
        As if by that alone she let all trouble go.

LONG DISTANCE IN ASIA MINOR

What if I call her long distance
To ask if her behind, like mine,
Had tingled in the night.

"No," she'd say, "it must be you alone
Sat on the power spot, never washed,
Never combed by the light of the moon.

Yet hear I did, from that secret church
Scooped by monks from a tufa cone
To house their barnacled Greek beliefs,

A grasshopper whistle, unique, unique,
Moon for dear life wallop her tom tom.
Sensing heaven in earth I did behold

The star burst, and was there, all of a piece,
When the wave rose and, cresting,
Compelled the skin you scratch –

For reasons, perhaps, electromagnetic –
To crack under the torture of the mundane...
For a syntax of God, turn, turn the fruit of time."

Who'd lark with a person so connected?
Back to its cradle the telephone, once
Hooked, hung loose, swung a little.

A VERY THIN MAN

Hearing tell one day of the Poseidonians,
He noted a kinship between those people
And the obscure selves that swarmed in his skin.
He felt their fingers poke through the fabric
Isolating him, throats crooned: to his spiritual
The indigo surge below the melody line.

The Poseidonians had been swallowed up
By an alien civilization. Greeks,
They had forgotten Greek, but still spoke
Or sang it, on occasion, when satisfied.
At festivals, or soon after lights went down,
They uttered words their life had sucked all sense from.

The fingers wanted something.
They wanted to go back among the skins
Of leopard, or of mole; back to ores
Still engrossed in rock; out or on to forces
Not yet connected in a form. His tongue
Would follow the fingers, and elide
With the grain dilating mahogany trees,
Conform to laws occult
In flocks of small birds when they turn.

Ridiculous how the man, if so much as a candle flame
Licked with its light the shoulder
Of a full wine bottle, began
To hear flutes and catch notes lower still,
Plucked on a lyre, stooped and ran for the crown
In a contest of one, for now, no longer
Pressed by any other selves, solo,
It was his breath exhaled the finish line.

SPHINX

Whenever a cat happened to die in Egypt,
People close to it shaved their eyebrows off:

What intimate rites of passage were these?
Did the hieroglyph for cat resemble,

Near enough, the eyebrow hieroglyph?
Think of those bushed and sleek

Eyebrows the Egyptians had. Imagine
The compassion, busy with a razor,

Black obsidian deftly worked across
The arched sockets of Egyptian eyes,

The vault of a cat's back collapsing –
Time for an eyebrow to breathe its last.

I see a tabby stroll, supple in his stripes,
Behind a bush, on ordinary grass:

Watch the lines of life ripple on his back,
And call to him with a human mouth.

It hardly matters if the cat is not a fine
Old ancestor, come back again; I only comprehend

How fragile he must be to walk at all,
Vigilant, every nerve elastic as the light.

So if he answers, I, like an Egyptian,
Take no chances, stand to be recognized:

We walk together on the same thread
Spun out and ringed by ignorant meows,

Manifold, for the embroiderer's drum excites
On our horizon scores of liquid pictures,

Taut as a bowstring bitten lips have wetted
In anguish. How else crouches the colossal

Cat, rooted in earth, scanning stars that promise
To spill a fish – and does without. Sacrifice

Is an act can weigh in the scale for a cat:
Sacrifice, to placate, when up it arches,

Torn apart, this flesh, in fury, speaks to spirit,
Loses the thread, and falls to paradise.

SONNET OF THE FAINT HEART

He loves to be in touch, that above all;
So when his time has come and he must die –
Intimates tiptoe round the bed and sigh –
He says they should put off his burial

A day or two, or three, if possible.
Then the dark visitors – to catch his eye,
Him being set to know what's what and why,
Is hard – they briefly nod and off they haul.

Yet such effusion of respect he takes
To differ not a bit from what he knew.
It's like the palping he's accustomed to:

A glance, bereft of obligation, rakes,
From random spectres squeaking past, the few
Sharp featured icons even he forsakes.

(Variation on a theme by Marin Sorescu)

THE TREASURE

So this is Iztuzu. The huge blue bay,
Craggy headlands, facing west-south-west.
Turtles bury eggs in the brown sandflats;
For ninety million years *caretta caretta*
Have known the place, have hatched here.

She wept, she said, for the beauty of it.
I take my stand halfway across, on a spit,
And harken to goats nattering among rocks:
Their long jaws bring lips to a meal of leaves.
She had wept for the beauty of it.

And then, then she happened on
A big shut seashell, rattled it, broke the seal
And picked from the dried muck in its hollow
A godsend, from the spirit of the place:
Six old gold Lykean coins.

Exactly where? Organ keyboard waves roll in,
The bay glistens, wind without a bird.
Down again to the beach, through sharp rocks,
I tango and think of the woman weeping,
Red henna hair and not yet stout.

The coins, lost for twenty five centuries,
Found by the woman who wept her heart out;
I will make do with a small white stone,
Shape of a snail on the march, a pocket Arp;
Silk shadow cooling a span of ground,

That there grasshopper will do for a dragon.
Back among beach huts I look to the pines:
Green slope, two flat cabins nesting on it;
Signs of a spring. Was it there she wept?
O turquoise nave of the bay's radiant amethyst!

I will make do with the stone in my pocket.
Ready to go, soon a rough gust, wind rising,
I see a shroud of dusty sand blown off the beach
Toward this bus, and wonder: What if the wind
Has bared a clutch of big shut seashells now?

CYPRESS AT THE WINDOW: A LETTER TO LOTTEN

A sort of cypress reached
Halfway up the window;
I came to live here, all the same.

Seldom visited by birds,
More often by chameleons,
It fills the window now.

Disheartening any window cleaner,
It filters dust and south light,
A permanent winter dream.

Yet if I go, evenings, to the door
In August, while I cross the room
It's me soaks up the shadow of the tree.

And I remember it was small: on the floor
We sat, if you remember, Lotten,
Watching, flake by flake, the snow

Cascade over, through, and round
The cypress, in a safe place.
The snow was rare and fell thick,

Whitest on the ground, for interposed
Green, like a whisper in the dark, is buoyant.
Now in the wind it sways, dusky thing,

And if hot light still floods the south,
The shadow of it whisks across the wall
Where camels loiter, silhouetted, in a desert.

Camel humps with saddle bows ink the dunes,
Alongside the shadows of their drivers.
The shadow of the cypress, waving, also

Includes my skin, now a sort of cloak;
I feel it in the desert for the first time
Lightly rustle round the shadow's tree.

Supposing, Lotten, you can catch
In Stockholm shadows that prolong,
Northward, articulating it, the violet

South, to swivel east
As fold on fold, reversed,
The desert veers away

And forges west, through snow, remember
How lightly for an hour you felt
The shadow rise, the growing tree.